T0099897

A
CHRISTIAN'S BOOK
of HAIKU

Daphne Washington

WESTBOW
PRESS
A DIVISION OF THOMAS NELSON

WestBow Press books may be ordered through booksellers or by contacting:

WestBow Press
A Division of Thomas Nelson
1663 Liberty Drive
Bloomington, IN 47403
www.westbowpress.com
1-(866) 928-1240

ISBN: 978-1-4497-5058-9 (sc)
ISBN: 978-1-4497-5059-6 (hc)
ISBN: 978-1-4497-5057-2 (e)

Library of Congress Control Number: 2012908397

Printed in the United States of America

WestBow Press rev. date: 8/29/2012

DEDICATION

For Joe, Joseph, and Jadon

Contents

Epigraph	ix
Preface	xi
Acknowledgments	xv
Academic Success	1
Financial Stewardship	31
Leadership	43
Finding Purpose	57
Grief	71
Overcoming Temptation	77
Mental and Spiritual Well-Being	81
Submission	105
Dreams	109
Self-Reflection	119
Children	129
Marriage	133
Family	139
Gratitude	141
Theology	153
Prayer	167
Encouragement	175
Afterword	189
About the Author	191
Resources	193

EPIGRAPH

Real haiku is the soul of poetry.
Anything that is not actually present in one's heart
is not haiku.
—Santōka Taneda

If we wish to consider haiku
as composed of perceptions and silences,
the latter are the more potent for evoking insight and awareness.
—Robert Spiess

PREFACE

Accepting the call:

allowing oneself to write

and express one's voice.

To proclaim yourself a writer, you must simply begin your vocation by committing yourself to a regular regimen of writing. That writing may start by taking various forms. Consistently engage in the process of putting thoughts on paper while also letting your creativity have a place of expression. Not only will you gain a sense of what you want to write about, but you will also gain greater clarity about how you would like to share your voice with the world.

When I decided to accept my call as a writer in the summer of 2011, I had a number of ideas in my head. I also had quite a bit of uncertainty about where to focus my energies and how to organize my thinking into a completed manuscript. As I put thoughts to paper, I saw topics emerge that spoke to roads I have traveled as well as roads that I am currently traveling. I found myself increasingly interested in guiding and encouraging students to promote their academic success. I thought of principles that would help me develop my own financial fitness plan for the upcoming year. I reflected on the blessings children are in our lives. I was reminded of the sanctity of marriage and its ministerial call. Wisdoms emerged to promote leadership, purposeful living, and mental and spiritual well-being. Numerous ideas reaffirmed my faith as well as my desire to encourage others to develop their relationships with God.

With so many different directions that I could pursue, I was looking for guidance in figuring out where my passions were the strongest. Surfing the Internet, I arrived at a Web site that focused on haiku. This Japanese form of poetry intrigued me. While I appreciated the artistry in which many of these poems spoke to the revelations found in nature, the mathematical side of me was caught by the five-seven-five syllabic rhythm of the poems. I was also impressed by how much could be beautifully stated with the brevity of seventeen syllables. I began to wonder how many of the ideas in my head could be expressed within this poetic form. And from this place, *A Christian's Book of Haiku* was born.

As you read this book, you will notice that the poems are grouped into topics. However, as you read through the haiku, do not be surprised if you notice that a particular haiku addresses more than just the topic under which it is listed. You may also see similar ideas expressed in more than one chapter through different haiku. The chapters are provided simply as starting points to easily locate a group of haiku related to a topic.

How you enjoy this book is up to you. While I was working on this manuscript, I found myself rereading some of the haiku at various times for my own personal encouragement, affirmation, and accountability. I would occasionally pick a haiku and meditate on it. At other times, I simply enjoyed the beauty of seeing ideas expressed in this brief, poetic form.

I titled this compilation of poems *A Christian's Book of Haiku* because I believe that my Christian journey deeply informs the writings found within. At the same time, I believe people of varying faith backgrounds may find a number of the ideas presented within the haiku helpful. For those readers who are also Christians, I encourage you to allow the haiku to stimulate Bible study; search the Scriptures to see what God's Word says about the ideas presented.

It is my hope that you are richly blessed by this work and that it becomes a welcome addition to your library.

Acknowledgments

First and foremost, I would like to give thanks to my Lord and Savior, Jesus Christ. It is in Him that my life gains purpose, and I am thankful for the many ways He encourages me to step out of my comfort zone and try new endeavors.

I would also like to give special thanks to the entire team at Westbow Press for their tremendous assistance in publishing this work. I am especially grateful to Donovan Gerken, who provided significant feedback and believed in the value of my writing before I did; and to Sarah Goddard, who gently and patiently walked me through a critical stage of the publishing process.

Finally, I would like to thank all of you who have supported me in my pursuit of this work. Special acknowledgments go to Dr. Joy Hervey, Christine Hollins, Dr. Harold Hunter, Dr. Mera Kachgal, LaShona Sellers, Dr. Diane Strike, Joseph Washington, Venice Washington, and Gail Waterhouse for their beneficial feedback and encouragement that aided me in bringing this manuscript to completion.

ACADEMIC SUCCESS

Study! Please study!

Study to prepare yourself

for God's ordained work.

~

Give your very best.

Feel God watching you always,

and study for Him.

Read course documents

at the start of your classes.

Know what's expected.

—

Expect to excel.

Believe you will have success,

and walk in that faith.

Make the sacrifice:

What must I give up for this?

Decide and let go.

~

Manage your time well.

Protect those precious time blocks.

Use them for learning.

Know what deters you.

Move away from distractions.

Move toward what feeds you.

—

Admit your weakness,

then seek help to address it.

It won't defeat you.

Exhaust resources.

Use what's at home, school, and work.

Make it work for you.

~

Know your supporters:

those who want to lift you up

and cheer when you win.

Coaching's also good.

We all need encouragement.

Get it where you can.

—

Know your professors.

Ask lots and lots of questions.

Ask and you'll receive.

Find study buddies:

those in the same boat as you

with the same end goal.

~

Get tutoring too;

one more smart way to get help.

Don't just spin your wheels.

And library skills?

You will need those—online too!

Ask librarians.

How's your computer?

It's necessary these days.

Keep it up to date.

Technical problems.

Unavoidable, it seems;

expect and prepare.

—

Computers do crash.

Power's out, the Web freezes.

Breathe—go with the flow.

Is your work backed up?
Let that extra copy bring
the gift of sweet peace.

—

Computer access.
You need to have more than one.
Can you access three?

Start papers early.

Count the cost and plan your time.

Don't procrastinate.

~

Enjoy your research.

Let it teach you something new

and build up your mind.

When writing papers,

remember: draft and edit,

then format for style.

—

Never plagiarize—

turning in someone else's

work as if it's yours.

Plagiarism hurts.

You may doubt the skills you have—

lost integrity.

—

Get some extra eyes

to review what you've written.

Then use the critique.

Know your learning style.

What helps you grasp the coursework?

Adapt as needed.

~

Do you listen well?

Make sure you can hear the text.

Then hear it again.

Does writing help you?

Take lots and lots of good notes.

Ask your books questions.

~

Are you a mover?

Listen and exercise too.

Get fit and get smart!

Need to make it plain?

Think how it applies to life.

Make it meaningful.

~

How do you refuel?

Do you spend daily prayer time?

Give thanks and sing praise?

Are you sleeping well?

Yes, students need to sleep too.

Get plenty of it.

~

When you feel tired,

remind yourself it's normal.

Get rest and move on.

There's a time for work,

as well as a time for rest.

Work hard and rest well.

⁓

Are you having fun?

Balancing your work with play

that nourishes you?

Tests have you nervous?

Are you praying before them?

How about during?

~

Nothing will defeat

what God has for you to do.

Trust, and believe that.

Daily devotions.

Are you spending time with God

absorbing His Word?

~

Focus on Scripture.

What does it say about you

and God's promises?

Hold on to God's Word—

even tighter when it's hard.

Let it sustain you.

~

You can use your mind

and believe in Jesus too.

Just know your limits.

Learn through studying—
not just the subject matter,
but how to excel.

~

Learning to excel
is a life skill that will bless
you abundantly.

Is your life balanced?

God's study does not neglect

those whom you're called to.

—

Teach that which you learn.

Sharing knowledge with others

builds your mastery.

Don't wait to finish.

Use your gifts while you study.

Serve with humbleness.

———

Let God shine through you

so that others will see you

yet be awed by Him.

When life throws a twist

that knocks the wind out of you,

pause, and then press on.

—

Run the race with pace.

Don't burn yourself out in haste.

Persist with patience.

Grades don't define you.
Occasionally, success
comes after failure.

～

Failure births success?
Yes—failure will help you see
your true commitment.

Sometimes we must fail

to build up our persistence

and test our motives.

~

Failure purifies.

It also can be humbling.

See the good in it.

Success is sweeter

when you work for it and win.

Remember that truth.

~

Seek to see past now.

That which you are now learning

sets your godly stage.

FINANCIAL STEWARDSHIP

What is a steward?

A caretaker of God's gifts:

both people and things.

—

Bills, bills, and more bills!

What's financial stewardship,

and how does it work?

What are extra bills?

Bills for items you don't need.

Cancel those bills first.

~

Sitting on money?

How can you sell and scale back?

Sell, sell, sell it now!

How is your spending?

Do you pay extra for things?

Why? Buy goods wisely.

~

Is what you're buying

hurting your walk with the Lord?

If so, don't buy it.

Are you indulging?

Does what you buy nourish you—

or does it numb you?

~

Try a spending fast:

Take a break from spending on

that which has control.

It could come as a

coffee, sweet, suit, shoe, gadget ...

It's led by impulse.

~

In that one moment,

you may feel you must have it,

but you really don't.

Don't make the purchase.
Instead, talk to God about
how you are feeling.

—

What's inside of you
prior to swiping your card?
What feeds the impulse?

Let Him heal that part.

And, wow! Before you know it

the impulse is gone.

~

And then, guess what else?

You'll now have extra money

that you can use well.

Do with what you have

in a way that makes God smile,

and you will be blessed.

—

Still need more money?

How does your work ethic look?

Are you wasting time?

Use all of your gifts.

None are too great or too small.

God provides through them.

—

Do not dread working.

Instead, do what you're made for.

That work fuels your life.

—

Poor in money is

opportunity to be

richer in spirit.

Lots of money can
destroy spiritual wealth
when handled wrongly.

—

What is recession?
Opportunity to shift
from money to God.

—

Can I be wealthy?
Absolutely! However,
invite godly wealth.

Godly wealth blesses.

It enriches others' lives.

It breaks away chains.

~

Real good stewardship

comes from remembering that

it is all from God.

~

What God gives to you

can grow your relationship

to Him. Just let it.

LEADERSHIP

Love others enough

to follow God without doubt.

Lead others to Him.

~

God is leading me,

but I am afraid of where.

It's okay. Show up!

Lord, may I face fears,

not run away cowardly.

May I approach them.

—

Do I leave my friends,

my family that I love?

When God says so, yes!

Loyalty to God:

Nothing is to be higher.

Not one thing at all.

~

To lead someone else,

you must first govern yourself

with self-discipline.

Teach on your growth edge.
It holds you accountable
and purifies you.

—

There is no moment
in which you're invisible.
You're seen at all times.

God always sees you,

and holds you accountable

for all that you do.

—

How does being seen

change the things you do and say?

Fosters self-control.

Do not fear greatness.

It's what you're created for.

Embrace it and soar!

—

God wants us to reign,

yet we may have to claim space

for that to occur.

Be your best right now!

Do not wait for someone else

to say it's okay.

~

Take time to reflect.

Don't get caught up day-to-day.

Seek to soar above.

Gain new perspective

in the moment of stillness.

Transcendent wisdom.

~

Do something that's new.

Don't be afraid to stand out.

Then try, try again.

Outside of the box—

there you will find direction.

Break the tradition.

—

Walk in God's freedom;

freedom to soar, risk, and live,

undefined by man.

—

What's walking in faith?

Choosing to live by God's Word

and not man's worldview.

Those who have gone through

are prepared to help others.

Authenticity.

—

Your pains and heartaches

have sensitized you more to

the pain of others.

—

Leaders can bless them.

Those who caused the greatest pain,

you can love in peace.

You can truly love

when God's love is flowing through.

Resistance is fear.

~

Good leaders listen

to the ones they are leading,

that they may breathe life.

~

Temper your feelings.

Do not let them run the show.

They're not good leaders.

Look beyond one's faults.

See past one's circumstances.

Relate heart-to-heart.

⁓

Always walk humbly.

Be quick to say I'm sorry,

and watch God's hands work.

⁓

How to be loving:

Feel God's presence in the room

and respond to it.

How to show respect:
Imagine God in the face
of those you are with.

〜

God calls youth to lead.
He knows exactly what you
are capable of.

〜

You are not too young.
Are you reading this haiku?
Then you're not too young.

FINDING PURPOSE

You're not a mistake.

You just don't know your purpose.

Ask the one who does.

~

Why am I this way,

in this skin and this body?

For God's unique plan.

You—unlovable?

Hard to believe God loves you?

But He does, He does!

~

What the world may mock,

God uses for His glory.

He sees true beauty.

Self-esteem in God:

a wonderful creation.

Nothing changes that.

—

I don't quite know me

in the purpose you made me.

Introduce me, please.

God introduces

us to ourselves through trials

that appear too great.

~

Trials are the fire

that makes the diamond appear

in all its splendor.

Look in the mirror.

Look beyond the pain and hurt.

See God's creation.

~

Then keep your eyes fixed.

Gaze deeply into God's love

and be awed by it.

Where is my breakthrough?
When I am right on the edge,
falling into God.

—

We will never gain
that which we could fully be
left to our own will.

What God thinks of you

will have all of the power.

His love never fails.

—

He builds character;

reshapes our priorities;

focuses our lives.

I am forgiven.

My frailties—depravities

don't cancel God's faith.

—

Yes, God sees it all

and uses it all for good.

In Him, you succeed!

In newness comes life.

Do not look back to the old;

it paralyzes.

~

God is always there,

replacing what's given up.

Transforming. Healing.

Embrace the purpose.

Put it on like new garments.

Leave the old behind.

~

Focus on the end—

the godly goal that's revealed.

The new strength coming.

Let Him make it known,

and then walk just as you are.

The past fades away.

~

As you look above

and experience God's truth,

you will be renewed.

God gifts His people.

Use your gifts to His glory.

Bless. Heal. Deliver.

—

Never doubt God's plan.

It's perfect, yet misconstrued.

Trust. He works through you.

GRIEF

Sadness will present.

Grief is inevitable.

Accept it and grow.

~

Loss of a loved one?

Feel the pain of one's absence.

Relish memories.

Look at one's pictures
if it will help you to grieve
and to remember.

~

There is life and death.
The existence of them both
brings meaning to each.

When one life ceases,

it can remind us of where

we are not living.

~

Within memories

are clues to your own freedom—

your present journey.

Where they had power,

you may become powerful,

flying on their backs.

—

Where they were real weak,

you may be prompted to grow,

to bring love and change.

Our loved ones want life

for those who are left behind.

Honor them and live.

～

Overcome! Excel!

Honor them with your success.

Remember their best.

～

Revere your loved ones

by building upon their strengths.

They helped to build you.

OVERCOMING TEMPTATION

What can ensnare you?

That which weakens your power

and your thirst for God.

~

Ah, pleasures of life—

so intoxicating and

blinding when indulged.

~

Yet fully enjoy

life, but sober and watchful,

focusing on God.

Know what entraps you.

Do not judge it or yourself.

Turn from temptation.

—

When you are caught up,

you will know the world has you.

Admit it. Be still.

—

Overestimate—

you cannot win on your own.

You aren't that strong.

Our minds are tempted.

Guard them with God's Holy Word.

It is our weapon.

~

Do not make a choice

solely based on your feelings.

Choose led by God's Word.

~

Remember your faith.

Walk not in what you can see,

but in your belief.

MENTAL AND SPIRITUAL WELL-BEING

Self-care in the Lord:

praying and staying in tune;

listen and follow.

~

Oh, your blessed Word—

soothes my weary mind and soul,

gives me hope and peace.

Are you filled with rage?

Be still and sit in silence.

Wait for it to pass.

—

Do not make a choice

solely based on your feelings.

They change too quickly.

Impulsivity—

oh, what trouble it may bring.

Pause before acting.

~

When something hurts you,

take the time to talk to God.

He will help you through.

No one is left out

from pain, hurt, and injustice.

You are not lessened.

~

Respond, not with wrath,

but with great humility.

This will honor you.

True forgiveness is
choosing to still love others
after they hurt you.

~

Let go of grudges.
Bitterness will destroy you.
Forgive and gain peace.

May we accept this:

Receive His true forgiveness,

and walk without shame.

—

Live in forgiveness.

Don't let shame dominate you.

Give smiles to yourself.

Move with God's current.

It may change so suddenly.

Fight and go under.

—

Depression equals:

trying to do it yourself

and not seeking help.

When you feel hopeless,
think of times you felt that way
and life turned around.

~

The seasonal blues.
The cloudiness that's outside
invites reflection.

Anxiety is:

forgetting God is with you,

and living in fear.

～

When you are fearful,

trust in the God that you serve.

Stand upon His Word.

What is acting out?

Desiring attentiveness

while feeling anxious.

—

Ridicule and fear:

They occur in parallel.

Fear not; you mock not.

The joy of the Lord,

resting in His holy love.

Hallelujah! Yes!

~

Can you rest in God?

Really rest; lay in His arms.

Let Him hold you now.

In God's arms is peace.

Healing that releases tears,

tears that lead to joy.

———

Tears are healing streams,

washing away pain and hurts

with restoration.

Do not fear your tears.

They will not flow endlessly

and will purify.

~

So amazing, Lord!

Yesterday's tears turn to joy.

Broken, then strengthened.

Periods of doubt

wracked with pain and much sadness

precede great breakthroughs.

—

Living in God's will,

there will be some pain involved.

Pain can mature us.

Lord, help me feel pain.

Then, I ask you to grow me

that I may persist.

~

Pain has such a sting.

So often I'd rather run

than to learn through it.

Pain alone won't kill.

It alerts us to problems;

problems God can solve.

—

To let go of pain,

you must trust in God's justice

and His redemption.

We can't fix others.

Ah, but the God we serve can;

just partner with Him.

~

Remember one thing:

What you think needs to be fixed

may not be broken.

And what needs healing,
you may not readily see,
but God can see it.

~

He does what serves all,
not governed by selfishness
or what soothes the flesh.

It is easy to

express one's thoughts in wrong ways.

Wrong is unhelpful.

~

Tame your tongue, the sword.

So easily can it wound

and inflict great hurt.

When you talk out loud,

you can hear what you're thinking,

and gain conviction.

~

So, confront your words.

Ask God to combat weak thoughts

and replace with life.

As one thinks he is,

that is what he will become.

Think grand, holy thoughts.

~

Connect with yourself.

Feel everything that's within.

Say only what heals.

Speak with compassion.

Speak with honesty, mercy.

Speak what must be said.

~

Seek to live in peace,

not in turmoil and conflict.

Speak calm, and turn toward it.

Speak abundantly.

Believe for prosperity.

See beyond the now.

~

The gift of our words.

May we use them to bring light

and to share God's love.

SUBMISSION

What is submission?

In exact terms—define it:

trusting God knows best.

—

Yes, God knows the way

that brings life, peace, joy, and strength,

if only we trust.

God's shackle gives life.

It does not take it away.

It restrains evil.

~

In humility,

there we gain our true freedom;

in true submission.

DREAMS

What is in a dream?
Insight that gives direction
for daily living.

~

Within submission,
we serve a God that wants to
fulfill godly dreams.

I am so angry.

I'm holding on to my dreams.

God, give me your dreams.

—

Not my will, dear Lord,

but thy will be done, correct?

Release dreams of flesh.

God uses flesh dreams.

Yet these are not for pursuit.

Pursuit stymies growth.

—

Remember your dreams.

Write them with great diligence

and expect wisdom.

Dreams represent you.
Each character is a glimpse
into your psyche.

—

Do not be afraid.
The most gut-wrenching of dreams
has something to give.

Sometimes dreams prompt prayer.

Pray for who you dream about.

It may be your call.

~

When you pray your dreams,

pray for the outcome God wants

based upon His Word.

And here's the blessing—

when you pray for those you dream,

you are also healed.

~

Dreams are like stories.

The Bible is full of them;

divine ones of truth.

Dreams in parallel

with a biblical story

aren't to be ignored.

—

Instead, study them.

Meditate on those stories,

and watch God guide you.

If you can dream it,

you can access what you need

to reveal its gifts.

—

Exercise patience.

God may reveal a vision

that's decades away.

SELF-REFLECTION

Search my heart, dear Lord.

Reveal wrong motivations.

Cleanse my ill-thinking.

—

Seek to see through God.

Use His eyes as your glasses.

Change your perspective.

It's hard to admit

we need to be guided by

much more than ourselves.

~

If we're not careful,

we'll run from that truth, and find

ourselves walking dead.

What do you attract?

Look at what is around you.

It's your reflection.

—

Who does your life please?

Is it God or is it man?

Man will not save you.

Reflect on your life.

Give yourself permission not

to engage in sin.

⁓

Prune, prune, prune your life.

Don't let it grow unruly.

Cut back. Trim. Cut off.

What would Jesus say

if He walked into your home?

How would your life change?

～

No one knows the day.

No one knows the exact hour.

Live as if it's now.

What makes up your thoughts?

Is your mind being renewed,

or clouded with doubt?

—

Do you talk too much,

using words without caution?

Measure what you say.

Examine yourself.

Words can be our hurts launched out.

Gather your swords first.

⁓

What pain drives your words?

What drives your actions and thoughts?

Identify it.

Are you conscious yet?

Do you know what real love is?

Can you receive it?

—

Life's tribulations—

God's soul laboratory.

How can this mold me?

CHILDREN

Children are a gift.

They love us, teach us, help us.

Catalysts for growth.

—

All children are blessed,

no matter what precedes them

or follows their births.

May we value them—

caring for them like fine jewels;

nourishing their souls.

~

Let children lead you.

Listen to the words they say.

Hear their small voices.

Learn from your children.
Blaze a bright path for them by
being what they need.

—

The path you create
for your children to walk down
mirrors who you are.

—

Bless your dear children.
Their lives bring the life-giver
healing, peace, and joy.

Marriage

Marriage teaches love;

how to love another soul

the way God loves us.

—

Look at Hosea

and God's choice for his partner.

What is God saying?

Marriage commitment:

not to be taken lightly;

a vow before God.

~

Love obligation:

One cannot divorce from that.

It is eternal.

Is marriage easy?

Nothing that's blessed comes easy.

All marriage takes work.

—

Yet, it's worthwhile work.

It's a divine mystery

that transforms you both.

Married and selfish—

these words can't go together

and heal a marriage.

—

Married and serving—

when you serve each other's needs,

marriage is strengthened.

FAMILY

Create family:

those who love you and you love,

both blood and spirit.

—

Oh, how blessed we are

to have others to travel

with on life's journey.

—

Learn from your elders.

Honor their lives with the way

you choose to live yours.

GRATITUDE

Count all your blessings.

Count them every single day.

Then change your outlook.

⁓

Give thanks to the Lord.

Praise Him with your whole being:

mind, body, and soul.

What I'm thankful for:

grace—favor I don't deserve.

God's blessed presents.

~

What I'm thankful for:

health, strength, wisdom, and vision.

God, family, friends.

What I'm thankful for:
my children and godchildren,
who push me to grow.

～

What I'm thankful for:
the gifts of our ancestors.
Strengths inherited.

What I'm thankful for:
the people God allows to
affirm who we are.

—

What I'm thankful for:
awareness that God loves me
despite all my faults.

What I'm thankful for:
adversities that opened
me to taking help.

—

What I'm thankful for:
the antidote to helpless
that comes through worship.

What I'm thankful for:
the way God grants help to those
who will receive it.

~

What I'm thankful for:
intelligence while knowing
I don't know it all.

What I'm thankful for:
relationship with the God
who does know it all.

—

What I'm thankful for:
the simple pleasures of life
in food and nature.

What I'm thankful for:
the seasons of life—ups, downs
that build gratitude.

—

What I'm thankful for:
learning to set boundaries
and also feel peace.

What I'm thankful for:
second chances when we fail,
and what failure brings.

⁓

What I'm thankful for:
knowing how to gain power
after rejection.

What I'm thankful for:
belief that we are to rule
and reign on the earth.

~

What I'm thankful for:
discernment to separate
others' thoughts from mine.

What I'm thankful for:
discernment to separate
others' thoughts from God's.

＿

What I'm thankful for:
God never gives up on me,
even when I do.

＿

What I'm thankful for:
God doesn't limit blessings
to my scale of doubt.

THEOLOGY

The Bible is real.

It is not a fairy tale:

something that's made up.

—

Jesus, oh Jesus!

May we never doubt your life.

You're real and alive!

Jesus is coming;

coming again for His church.

Believe! Be ready!

~

Ponder this question:

If Jesus is not living,

why do souls react?

The earth testifies,

and science reveals its truth.

The rocks do cry out.

—

The proof's in nature.

In the witness of others.

In our history.

What is important—

where your soul will reside? Yes,

that is important.

⁓

Believe, yes believe!

This is not all that there is.

This is just the door.

Your prior beliefs

do not disqualify you.

Jesus loves us all.

～

What is irony?

Watching those who despise you

commit the same sins.

Christians are sinners.

When you see your sinful side,

bask in God's great love.

~

Sinners also soar.

Their wrongs don't disqualify.

Don't choose otherwise.

What causes illness?

The consequences of sin;

ours and those before.

—

Yes, it is finished,

but you must truly repent.

Walk in the newness.

Christians—not in name.

Be a Christian in belief.

Let your life show it.

~

In a world of change,

God's character does not change.

Never. Not ever.

Unlimited God.

Let that sink in really well …

Unlimited God.

⌒

Oh, how wonderful.

Oh, how perfect is your love.

Nothing surpasses.

You don't forget us.

Time moves on, but you're still there;

longing to return.

—

At life's finale

comes a great new beginning.

Remember! Hold on!

We have victory!

God leads us toward fulfilled life.

We follow and win!

—

Suffering will come.

Look to the cross for guidance,

strength, and renewal.

And we live in hope,

in great anticipation

of the good to come.

~

How to take preachers:

Listen with an open mind,

but hold to God's Word.

Dear Holy Spirit,

please guide us with your wisdom.

May we follow it.

～

Christ's diversity:

all races embraced in Him.

No segregation.

～

Christmas and Easter:

wonderful times of worship.

Birth. Resurrection.

PRAYER

Don't devalue prayer.

It is your link to divine.

The great connection.

—

In the stillness, pray.

Pour yourself out before God.

Ask for what you need.

—

Believe God hears you

and answers in the best way;

the way that gives life.

Ask, and it's given.

Believe, and you shall have it.

Receive your desire.

~

Whatever it is,

God can handle it with ease.

Anything. Just ask.

~

Listen for God now.

Listen for God all the time.

Expect to hear Him.

Know when God's speaking.

Learn to hear what His voice says,

and how He says it.

—

Sing! Sing! Sing your prayers!

Praise God with your lips and heart.

Music soothes the soul.

Yes, we have weakness.
Yet in weakness, we can praise
and then grow stronger.

—

Write out what's inside.
Pray with God about it too.
Use your mouth in love.

When you pray your pains,

you release healing power.

Place them in God's hands.

—

I whispered a prayer.

You answered me, and you said,

"I see you. Be free!"

When confusion comes,

Lord, may I speak honest prayers

that liberate me.

~

When you feel alone,

know that God is always there.

Talk to Him and trust.

Talk to God at night.

Talk to God during the day.

Talk to God always.

—

This is one huge hill.

Am I really in God's will?

Ask Jesus. Ask God.

—

Pray for the nations.

Politicians are not God.

Talk to the true King.

ENCOURAGEMENT

I may be tired,

ready to give it all up;

and yet God says, "No!"

~

When my flesh is done,

God's still steadily fighting,

encouraging me.

Crushed by life's struggles,

yet transformed by God's power.

Unstoppable love!

~

He loves us that much.

Nudging us through our trials,

growing and healing.

Love may not feel good,

yet love is fruitful and true.

Love will bring forth life.

⁓

That which may pain us,

God can use to strengthen us.

Allow Him, and heal.

Wow! How life can change—
one minute, so overwhelmed;
the next, ecstatic!

~

Feeling overwhelmed?
Unsure how this will play out?
God can handle it.

You are not alone;

even when it feels that way.

And you are covered.

~

Help that is removed

is an opportunity

to become greater.

What builds our patience?

That which makes us have to wait,

finding calm in storms.

~

Lord, please heal my wounds.

Yet in your perfect timing,

bring peace and renew.

In sickness comes rest.

Time to sit down and hear God;

gain redirection.

—

Rest in life's rhythm,

and maximize each season

and what it offers.

God is not confused.

Are you feeling overwhelmed?

Let God manage it.

~

Then move out, away.

Let God do what He does best.

He can take it on.

All is not perfect,

but I will keep pushing on.

God does not let go.

~

Please, trust and believe.

You are not alone in this.

God is by your side.

Look for God right now.

Look for His presence in life.

Expect to see Him.

⁓

What a blessed feeling—

see God in your darkest place,

coming just for you.

Go after blessings.

Don't allow shame to deter.

Press through and believe.

—

That which comes to light

has no power to destroy,

only to mature.

The absurd could be

the way to a real breakthrough.

May we discern it.

～

Bring on the thunder!

Shake the earth and flood my world.

Strengthen me in you.

AFTERWORD

Thank you for your love.

May you be blessed by this work,

and filled with great hope.

Thank you for the opportunity to share this compilation of poems with you. It is my hope that this book is the first of many. I would greatly appreciate hearing from you, the reader, to find out not only how the haiku are received, but also to learn more about you.

Please feel free to contact me and share what led up to receiving this book, your experience of the haiku, and your thoughts on other books that you would like to read in the future. You may e-mail me at dlbwashington@gmail.com or write to me at: Daphne Washington, 115 Wight Avenue #1491, Cockeysville, MD 21030. You also may visit my website at www.daphnewashington.com.

Be blessed.

ABOUT THE AUTHOR

Daphne Washington completed her Ph.D. at the University of Minnesota, Twin Cities. She majored in Educational Psychology, with an emphasis on Counseling and Student Personnel Psychology and a minor in Child Psychology. She also completed graduate studies in school guidance and counseling and biblical counseling at The Johns Hopkins University and Trinity Theological Seminary, respectively. Her professional experience includes service in university counseling, pastoral counseling, and Christian counseling settings. Daphne has also served as an educator for over sixteen years, ten of which have been in the field of distance education. She is currently an assistant professor of graduate counseling for Liberty University Online. Daphne has had a heart for writing for many years and fondly remembers receiving the English Award at her eighth grade graduation. During her adolescence, she published one poem entitled, "Love Without Words." She and her husband, Joseph, have been married close to fifteen years and live with their two sons in Maryland.

Resources

If you enjoy reading and meditating on haiku written from a Christian perspective, you may also appreciate the book, *Christian Haiku: The 17-Syllable Devotional* by Clark Osborn.

For more information about this book and the author, visit www.christianhaiku.com.